Fun-Schooling With Thinking

COUNTDOWN TO CHRISTMAS JOURNAL & COLORING BOOK

Coloring, Cooking, Poetry, Traditions, Games & Creativity

Poems By: Charity J. Thayer & Mimi Thayer
Produced By: Sarah Janisse Brown
Artwork By: Tanya Hulinska
Cover By: Sarah Brown
Published By: \The Thinking Tree Publishing
Company LLC Copyright 2016

December

Sunday	Monday	Tuesday	Wednesday	Thursday	Friday	Saturday

Day One

The Holidays are here, joyous Christmas is near!
Let's celebrate the happiest time of the year!
Snowflakes are dancing outside in the sky!
Children are taking their sleds out to ride!
What a wonderful feeling it is to know
That Christmas is near, when we see the first snow!

Now add your own words:

The Holidays are here, joyous Christmas is near!
Let's _____ the _____ time of the year!
_____ are _____ outside in the sky!
Children are taking their sleds out to ride!
What a _____ feeling it is to know
That Christmas is _____, when we see the first snow!

Gifts to Make or Buy:

_____
_____
_____
_____
_____
_____
_____
_____
_____
_____

A CHRISTMAS RECIPE

TIME TO BAKE

Penguin's Perfect Pumpkin Bread

1 Large Can Pumpkin
3 cups Sugar
¾ Cups Vegetable Oil
3 3/4 Cups of Flour
3 teaspoons Baking Soda
½ teaspoon Salt
1 teaspoon Cinnamon
½ Teaspoon Ground Cloves

Preheat Oven to 350.
Mix Pumpkin and Sugar Until Sugar is Dissolved.
Add Oil and Mix Well.
Mix the dry ingredients in a separate bowl.
Add Flour Mixture to Pumpkin Mixture and Mix Well.
Divide into 2 Loaf Pans.
Bake for 45 to 60 minutes or until toothpick inserted in the middle comes out clean.

NOTES:

_____
_____
_____
_____
_____
_____
_____
_____

Day Two

What a glorious time to gather with friends and family
There will be baking, gift giving and decorating the tree!
We will sing Christmas carols and make gingerbread
While we decorate our home in bright green and red!
We'll drink yummy hot cocoa with sticks of peppermint candy
And celebrate family traditions, with joy and merriment.

Now add your own words:

What a _____ time to gather with friends and family
There will be baking, _____ and decorating the tree!
We will sing Christmas _____ and make gingerbread
While we decorate our _____ in bright green and red!
We'll drink _____ with sticks of peppermint candy
And celebrate family traditions, with _____ and merriment.

Decorating Plans:

_____
_____
_____
_____
_____
_____
_____
_____
_____
_____
_____

Color Me!

Draw the missing parts!

Day Three

One of the most magical things about December,
Is that all month long there are fun times to remember!
Like going out with family for an evening drive
And seeing houses with colored lights shining bright.
Picking out special gifts and Christmas cards that we'll send
Or building a snowman with our two very best friends.

Now add your own words:

One of the most _____ things about December,
Is that all month long there are _____ to remember!
Like going out with the family for an evening _____
And seeing _____ with colored lights shining bright.
Picking out special _____ and Christmas cards that we'll send
Or building a _____ with our two very best friends.

Favorite Christmas Songs:

_____
_____
_____
_____
_____
_____
_____
_____
_____
_____

Caribou's Classic Chocolate Chip Cookies

2 1/4 cups all-purpose flour
1 teaspoon baking soda
1 teaspoon salt
1 cup (2 sticks) butter, softened
1 cup granulated sugar
1/2 cup packed brown sugar
1 1/2 teaspoon vanilla extract
2 eggs
1 package chocolate chips

PREHEAT oven to 350
Cream the Sugar and Butter until well mixed
Add Eggs and Vanilla, Mix well
In Separate Bowl Mix all Dry ingredients except Chocolate Chips
Mix the Dry ingredients with the wet ingredients, Mix well
Add Chocolate Chips and stir until well moistened
Drop Spoonful of Cookie Dough on Ungreased Cookie Sheet
BAKE for 7 - 8 minutes or until light brown
Cookies may appear undercooked but this is the secret to making them extra chewy and delicious.
Cool a minute or two before removing from cookie sheet.

NOTES:
_____
_____
_____
_____
_____
_____
_____
_____

Day Four

There are Christmas songs playing everywhere that we go
When we step outside there's the crisp smell of ice and snow.
So many lovely scents greeting us at Christmastime
Like cookies baking, cozy fires and wreaths made of pine.
A turkey roasting in the oven on Christmas day
Hot cocoa, peppermint and pumpkin pies as they bake!

Now add your own words:

There are Christmas songs playing everywhere that we go
When we step outside there's the crisp smell of _____.
So many lovely _____ greeting us at Christmastime
Like _____ baking, cozy fires and wreaths made of pine.
A turkey roasting in the oven on Christmas day
Hot cocoa, _____ and pumpkin pies as they bake!

Favorite Holiday Foods:

_____
_____
_____
_____
_____
_____
_____
_____
_____
_____

Color Me!

Draw the missing parts!

Day Five

We have family traditions we celebrate each year
As December begins and Christmas season draws near.
My family gathers to decorate the tall tree
We drink cocoa and pop popcorn to put on a string.
We hang tinsel, popcorn garlands, lights in bright colors
On our family tree, with all our sisters and brothers.

Now add your own words:

We have family traditions we celebrate each year
As December begins and Christmas season draws near.
My family gathers to decorate _____
We drink cocoa and pop _____ to put on a string.
We hang tinsel, popcorn garlands, _____ in bright colors
On our family _____, with all our sisters and brothers.

People to spend time with this season:

_____
_____
_____
_____
_____
_____
_____
_____
_____
_____

A CHRISTMAS RECIPE

Bunny's Best Banana Bread

1 ¼ Cup Sugar
½ Cup Butter Softened
2 Eggs
3 to 4 Very Ripe Bananas (Mashed)
¼ Cup Milk
¼ Cup Sour Cream
1 teaspoon Vanilla
2 ½ Cups Flour
1 teaspoon Baking Soda
1 teaspoon Salt

Heat Oven to 350
Grease Bottoms Only of 2 Loaf Pans
Mix Sugar and Butter in Large Bowl, Stir in Eggs until well blended
Add Milk, Sour Cream, Bananas and Vanilla
In separate Bowl mix the dry ingredients together
Add Dry ingredients to Wet Ingredients — Stir just until moistened
Bake Loaves about an Hour
Bread is finished when wooden pick inserted comes out clean
Let cool 5 or ten minutes before cutting
ENJOY!

NOTES:

_____
_____
_____
_____
_____
_____
_____
_____

Day Six

Through the house we hang garlands
Of sparkly gold, red, and green,
Then my dad plays guitar and we join in to sing,
We sing Christmas songs as the falling snow glistens.
Think of your favorite winter traditions!
We've been counting the days, can you hear the bells ring?
The big day is nearly here, let's all dance and sing!

Write the Words of your Favorite Christmas Song:

_____
_____
_____
_____
_____
_____
_____
_____
_____
_____
_____
_____
_____
_____
_____
_____
_____

Color Me!

Draw the missing parts!

Day Seven

We bake cookies and pies, we decorate gingerbread
With frosting and sprinkles of silver, gold, green & red!
We wrap festive presents in sparkly paper and bows
This part is very special because everyone knows
That by showing love and giving gifts
Is how we share the joy of Christmas.
By giving to others we reach out
To bring our joy to other faces!

Draw a gift that you want to give:

Color Me!

Draw the missing parts!

Day Eight

There'll be secrets, surprises and homemade gifts
Children have been hoping and making their lists!
Family arrives from faraway places
It is good to see our loved one's sweet faces!
Aunts, Uncles, Grandparents, and dear family friends
We share stories, laughter, and Holiday cheer.

Draw a picture of your family:

Color Me!

Draw the missing parts!

Day Nine

Time together is a precious gift sent down from above
The true meaning of Christmas is sharing, caring and love!
Christmas is a special season, unlike any other
Bringing families together for a time filled with wonder!

Add your own lines to the poem:

___
___
___
___
___
___
___
___
___
___
___
___
___
___
___
___
___
___
___
___
___

Owl's Oatmeal Cookies

1 cup Granulated Sugar
1 cup Brown Sugar (packed)
½ Cup Softened Butter
½ Cup Shortening
1 teaspoon baking Soda
1 teaspoon Cinnamon
1 teaspoon vanilla
½ teaspoon baking Powder
½ teaspoon salt
3 Medium Eggs
3 Cups Old Fashioned Oats
2 Cups Flour

Heat Oven 350 degrees
Cream the Sugar and Butter until well mixed
Add Eggs and Vanilla, Mix well
In Separate Bowl Mix all Dry ingredients except Oats
Mix the Dry ingredients with the wet ingredients, Mix well
Add Oats and stir until well moistened
Drop Spoonful of Cookie Dough on Ungreased Cookie Sheet
Bake 9 minutes or until light brown
Let Cool Before Eating
The Cookies will be chewy and delicious!

NOTES:

_____
_____
_____
_____
_____
_____
_____
_____

Day Ten

In the evening the sun sets and candles are lit
The Christmas tree shines bright, as together we sit
Around a cozy fire while snow starts to fall
Winter nights are the most magical nights of all.

Draw a Candle:

Color Me!

Draw the missing parts!

Day Eleven

Dad reads the Christmas story from our family Bible
He talks of Shepherds, Angels, and the Birth of the Child
Wise men on their camels with gifts following a bright Star
Angels singing in the skies to guide shepherds from afar
All are drawn to the straw manger where a new Baby lay
Oh how we all love the story of that first Christmas Day!

Look in the Bible for the story of the First Christmas and write a verse here:

_____
_____
_____
_____
_____
_____
_____
_____
_____
_____
_____
_____
_____
_____
_____
_____

Day Twelve

We drink hot cocoa with sticks of peppermint
Then each child may open one special present.
Loving Grandmas sit with babies on their knee
Brothers and sisters whisper excitedly.

Draw a picture of your favorite winter drink in a colorful mug:

Day Thirteen

We hang Christmas stockings by fire light
Say our prayers and kiss our parents goodnight.
We climb in to cozy beds as our excitement rises
For we know Christmas morning will be full of surprises!

Write your own Prayer:

_____
_____
_____
_____
_____
_____
_____
_____
_____
_____
_____
_____
_____
_____
_____
_____
_____
_____
_____
_____

Day Fourteen

Wake up! Wake up! When Christmas morning is here!!!
The joyful day we have awaited all year!!!
The sun is not up but the children will sneak
Down the hall so quiet to have a quick peek
At the presents piled up under the bright Christmas tree!
And stockings are overflowing with toys and sweet treats!

Add your own lines to the poem:

Day Fifteen

It's still dark outside but the fire is glowing.
And we are overjoyed to see that it's snowing!
The earth is covered with an icy layer of white
It is such a lovely bright Christmas morning sight!
Kids start peeking at presents and longing to see
Which ones have their names, wondering what they might be!

Draw a Winter Wonderland:

Day Sixteen

Children will open their stockings to find gifts, nuts and fruit
A new kitten with a big bow waits to greet them, **So Cute!**
Mom and Dad awake to hear children giggling as they play
Parents are also excited it is now Christmas day!
Family gathers as the morning sun begins to rise
Just to see all the joy reflected in the Children's eyes.

Draw a picture of a Christmas Kitten:

Day Seventeen

We give each other gifts, hugs, and thank one another
A doll house for sister, a train for little brother.
The baby laughs and plays with a shiny new ball
And Mom tears up to see the joy shared by them all.

Draw a picture to illustrate this poem:

Day Eighteen

Then the smell of cinnamon rolls may fill the air
As the kitten jumps in wrapping paper scattered everywhere.
Times like these remind us that we are truly blessed
As we make Christmas memories that we will never forget.

Draw a picture to illustrate this poem:

Day Nineteen

In the early afternoon we gather in the kitchen
Lots of cooking to do and the kids will pitch in
There's a turkey to stuff and potatoes to mash
Green bean casserole to mix and don't forget the sweet yams.

Christmas recipes and traditions are shared from mother to child
The kitchen is cozy with fresh savory scents that make us smile.
Mom always makes fresh bread and rolls
The table is set with Grandma's china plates, silverware, & bowls.
And then the most important part is that we gather once again
To share a special holiday meal with our family and friends.

Draw a picture to illustrate this poem:

Day Twenty

Grandpa may lead us in prayers and blessing
Then we pass around the potatoes and turkey dressing
We gather around the table, the kids can hardly wait
As Dad carves the Turkey and fills up each plate!
Such a precious time catching up with friends and relatives
Around the family dinner table on a day like Christmas.

Share a Memory about Christmas Dinner:
_____
_____
_____
_____
_____
_____

Draw your Memory:

Day Twenty-one

After dinner around the fire we'll gather
Children play with new toys, we share talk and laughter
There'll be coffee, cocoa, and pies topped with whipped cream
And the sunset on the white snow looks like a dream.

Share a Memory about Christmas Dessert:

_____
_____
_____
_____
_____

Draw your Memory:

Day Twenty-two

We have different traditions we share in our home
Each family has ways to celebrate all their own
There are so many holiday moments to fill us with pleasure
But the most important of all, is that we are all together.

Merry Christmas to Everyone, Let Love be the Reason
That we Gather Together and Celebrate this Season!

Share a Memory about a Christmas Tradition:

_____
_____
_____
_____
_____
_____

Draw your Memory:

Day Twenty-three

Families around the world have different ways
Of celebrating the wonderful Winter Holidays!
In some families the Christmas Tree is very important
With a story or memory behind each treasured ornament.
Some Christmas heirlooms are handed down for generations
While others are beautiful handmade children's decorations.
We unpack our ornaments with tender love and care
Enjoying each story and memory that we share.

Draw a Christmas Heirloom or Ornament:

Day Twenty-four
Christmas Eve - December 24th

Another way we pass down our fun family traditions
Are through special recipes that we share in our kitchens.
Some families make turkey, some make a ham
Some make special pies or cookies with sweet jam.

Some families make tamales or tasty mint pies
Some cook Lamb with mint jelly or old Welsh Rarebit Bites.
So many holiday recipes, all unique and delicious
What are some of your family's favorite cooking traditions?

Make a list of your favorite cooking traditions:

_____
_____
_____
_____
_____
_____
_____
_____
_____
_____
_____
_____
_____
_____
_____

Day Twenty-Five
Christmas Day! December 25th

Some families bake a very special Birthday cake
The birth of baby Jesus is what they celebrate!
There are many traditions we share in December
But this is the most important thing to remember!

It is the story we tell of Christ's Nativity
About how God came to earth as a helpless baby.
The angels and stars we carefully place upon our tree
Tell the story of the Savior who came to set us free.

So no matter how you celebrate this Holiday season
Remember that family and Jesus are the true reasons
That we gather together and exchange all our presents
Family and Christ's love are the true meaning of Christmas.

Draw a Nativity Scene or a Birthday Cake for Jesus:

Snowy Day Sugar Cookies
Easy No-Chill Recipe

1 cup butter
1 2/3 cups sugar
1 egg
2 teaspoons vanilla
2 3/4 cups all-purpose flour
2 teaspoons baking powder
1 teaspoon salt

Preheat oven to 375 degrees.
In mixing bowl, cream butter with sugar until light and fluffy. Beat in egg and vanilla.
Mix the rest of the ingredients in a separate bowl.
Add dry ingredients to wet ingredients 1 cup at a time, mixing after each addition.
No need to chill dough!
Divide dough into two balls. On a floured surface roll each ball into a circle approximately 12" wide and 1/8" thick.
Dip cookie cutter in flour and cut out cookies.
Bake on ungreased cookie sheet for 6 - 7 minutes or until cookies are lightly browned.
If you like you can line pans with parchment paper for easy cookie removal.

NOTES:

_____
_____
_____
_____
_____
_____
_____

Winter Journal & Christmas Planning
Date: _____

Winter Journal & Christmas Planning
Date: _____

Winter Journal & Christmas Planning
Date: _____

Winter Journal & Christmas Planning
Date: _____

Manufactured by Amazon.ca
Bolton, ON